J
54
MW01710998
JMC
DISCARDED

Wapiti regional library

# PAPER SCULPTURE

**John Lancaster**

Consultant: Henry Pluckrose

Photography: Chris Fairclough

9403660

FRANKLIN WATTS
London/New York/Sydney/Toronto

Copyright © 1989 Franklin Watts

Franklin Watts Inc.
387 Park Avenue South
New York
NY 10016

Library of Congress Cataloging-in-Publication Data

Lancaster, John, 1930–
Paper sculpture.

(Fresh start)
Includes index.
Summary: Provides step-by-step instructions on how
to make paper and create art objects by tearing, folding,
and weaving paper.
1. Paper—Juvenile literature. 2. Paper sculpture—Juvenile literature. [1. Paper work. 2. Paper sculpture. 3. Handicraft] I. Title. II. Series: Fresh start (London, England)
TT870.L255 1989 745.54 89–8887
ISBN 0-531-10758-2

Design: K & Co
Editor: Jenny Wood
Printed in Belgium

**Acknowledgement**
It gives me a great deal of pleasure to express my thanks to Mrs Joan Gaunt for her help in the preparation of this book, as well as to Jane Mansfield who produces hand-made papers in her workshop at Pentrecagal near Newcastle Emlyn in Wales. Jane sells small sheets of her papers – a few of which appear in one of the illustrations in this book, and demonstrates her paper-making techniques to visitors who are welcomed at her workshop. Henry Pluckrose and Chris Fairclough also have my thanks for their invaluable help.

John Lancaster

# Contents

# Equipment and materials

This book describes activities which use the following:

Bench (or work table, covered with a plastic sheet, old blanket or newspaper)
Ball (rubber ball or small soccer ball)
Brass or aluminum braces (four "L-shaped," size 1″ (2.5cm) or similar, and screws)
Cardboard (various kinds, including waste card)
Cardboard boxes (in which to store your equipment and paper)
Cold water dyes
Cork tile 12″ x 12″ (30cm x 30cm) felt or carpet square
Darning needle
Felt-tipped pens
Flower heads (also some petals, leaves and grasses)
Fork
Hammer
Jam jar (old)
Paper towels
Lemon
Nail 1″ or 2″ (2.5cm or 5cm)
Net curtain (or nylon material with fine or textured mesh)
Paint (water-based), or crayons
Paintbrushes (No. 5 or No. 7 watercolor brushes, and household paintbrushes)
Paper (a range of papers, including bought and scrap papers)
Pencil
Petroleum jelly (sold under the trade name "Vaseline")
Plastic bowl (for mixing paste)
Plastic buckets
Plastic washing-up bowl
Ruler (metal for use in cutting, and wooden)
Scissors
Screwdriver
Seeds (a variety of flower seeds, coffee grains, tea leaves, etc)
Shirt
Sponge
Spoons (a wooden spoon or strong stick for stirring, and an old metal spoon)
Stanley knife or "X-Acto" knife
Scotch tape
String
Thumbtacks (or a staple gun and staples)
Toothpicks
Wallpaper paste
Water
Wire baking rack (or similar wire object)
Wood (lengths of soft wood for making a mould, see pages 20-22)

# Getting ready



## What is paper?

Paper is a material we take very much for granted. We write, draw or paint on paper. When we go shopping, the articles we buy are usually put into paper bags. The books we read are printed on paper. How could we do without this simple yet special material?

It is thought that the art of papermaking originated in China two or three centuries before the birth of Christ. The name "paper" comes from the flat sheets which the Arab peoples of the Middle Eastern countries made from the stalks of the papyrus plant.

This book will show you one simple way of making your own paper from simple materials and with basic equipment. By making paper you will gain an understanding of the material itself and the process of its manufacture. You will then be shown how to use paper in different ways. This means that you will be able to experiment inventively in creating patterns, pictures and designs.

## Some hints

Cover your bench or work table with a large plastic sheet, an old blanket or sheets of newspaper.

Cover yourself, too, with an old shirt or smock.

Have ready your basic kit of materials and equipment (see page 4). Store them in a cardboard box.

**1** Keep your paper collection in a separate box. You could include old newspapers and magazines, cardboard egg cartons, colored tissue paper, used wrapping paper, scraps of wallpaper, old letters and envelopes, paper plates, paper towels and candy wrappings.

# Pricking paper

Sheets of paper which have had patterns or pictures pricked on them are most effective and interesting to look at. What you do is make small holes through the paper so that when you hold it up, the light hits the punctured areas and any parts of the surface which are raised.

You will need sheets of paper, a cork tile (or similar) on which to place your paper, a hammer, a nail, other pointed tools such as a screwdriver, darning needle, or pair of scissors, a toothpick, pencil and a ruler.

**1** Using the hammer and nail, make some holes in a sheet of paper. Go on to experiment with the other pointed tools.

**2** With the pencil (or felt-tipped pen) and the ruler, draw a series of straight lines across a sheet of paper.

**3** Punch holes along these lines with the screwdriver. Leave spaces between the holes.

**4** Draw freehand a series of circular shapes on another sheet of paper. With the screwdriver, prick holes through the paper along the lines you have drawn. Now turn the paper over to obtain a "reversed pattern" effect.

**5** Try painting the holes in some of your designs with a small brush and brightly-colored paint.

**6** Use a fork to see what kind of punctured holes it makes.

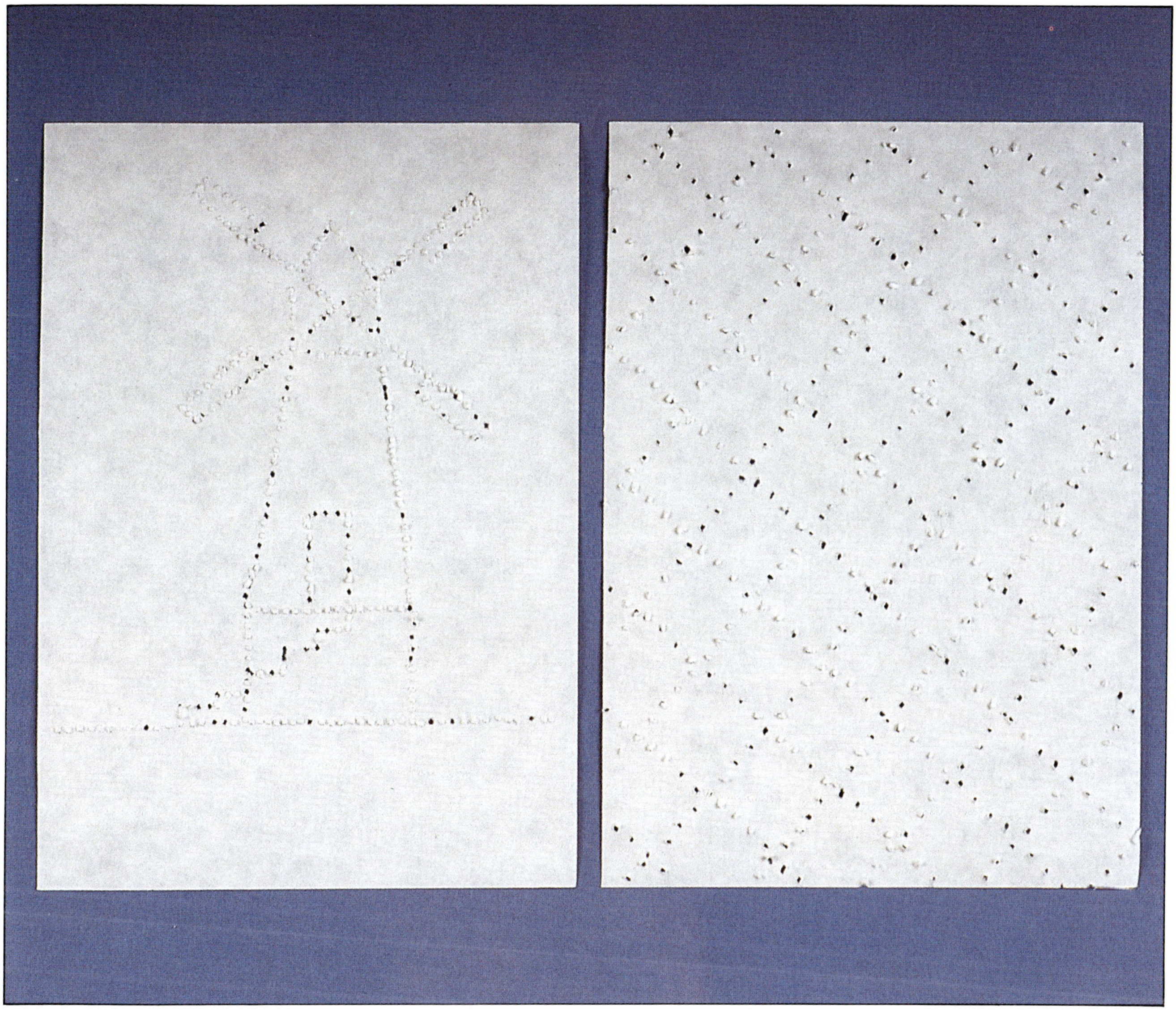

**7** Examples of pricked-paper patterns.

On a clean, brightly-colored piece of paper, make a great number of holes. Some of these could be fine holes (done with a needle) while others could be bolder (done with a screwdriver or nail), but they must be done in a "freehand" way. Hold your punctured paper pattern up to a light or a window. Try using colored tissue paper or colored cellophanes (candy wrappings would do nicely) to make your pattern more interesting.

# Tearing paper

Paper may be torn in a simple, freehand way. This produces "odd" shapes.

You will need a variety of types of paper, cardboard or tagboard.

**1** Practice tearing various paper shapes of different sizes. These might include shapes which are square; shapes which are very long and narrow; and shapes which are circular.

**2** Tear some long, thin strips of paper and glue these down on to a piece of cardboard to form an interlacing pattern.

**3** To ensure that this pattern is effective, use different colored papers or colored illustrations from magazines.

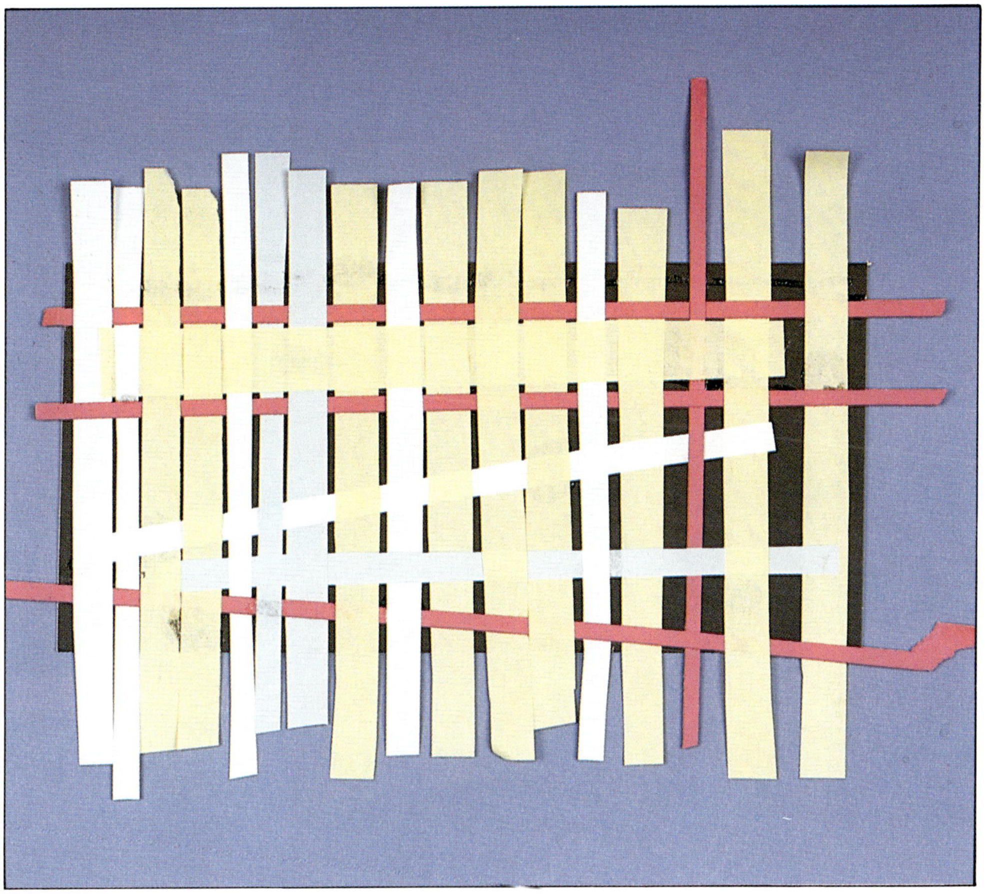

**4** *A useful hint*
In order to tear long, straight paper strips, lay your sheet of paper flat on your table or bench. Place the ruler on the paper where you intend to make the tear. Holding the ruler steady with one hand, pull the paper towards and against the ruler with your other hand.

Using different colored papers, try making paper collage pictures of, for example, a tree, a clown or a tractor.

# Crumpling paper

Almost any kind of paper may be crumpled in the hands. This is an effective way of producing interestingly textured areas for use in collage pictures or patterns.

You will need a variety of types of paper, cardboard or tagboard, glue, crayons or paints, a paintbrush, a jar of water, newspaper, heavy books, cold coffee, dye and kitchen towels.

**1** Crumple a piece of paper firmly in your hands.

**2** Unfold the paper and stick the top edge to a piece of cardboard. Push the rest of the paper around to form an interesting shape. Glue the rest of the paper down as well, in your chosen pattern.

**3** Color a sheet of paper with streaky marks, using crayons or dryish paint.

**4** Take this sheet and crumple it in your hands. Now crumple it twice more. This should give you a softer effect.

Another idea is to take three pieces of quite different types of paper and crumple each one firmly. Tear them into two or three pieces so that you have a number of smaller crumpled pieces. Now arrange them as a pattern on a sheet of cardboard and stick them down.

**5** Dampen a sheet of paper and then crumple it. Lay it on a pad of newspaper or paper towels and place a second pad on top. Now put a sheet of strong cardboard on top of this pad and weight it down with some heavy books. When it is dry, examine the crumpled paper to see what effects you have achieved. You could use these papers in a collage picture.

**6** Try dipping a tightly-crumpled ball of paper into some cold coffee or dye. When it has dried, open it out and you will have a crackled effect. Japanese papers sometimes have lovely "punctured" patterns and these can be stained in this way to make them even more interesting.

**7** Stick some of the pieces of paper which you have crumpled on to a strong sheet of colored paper or cardboard.

**8** You can arrange them so that they form a design.

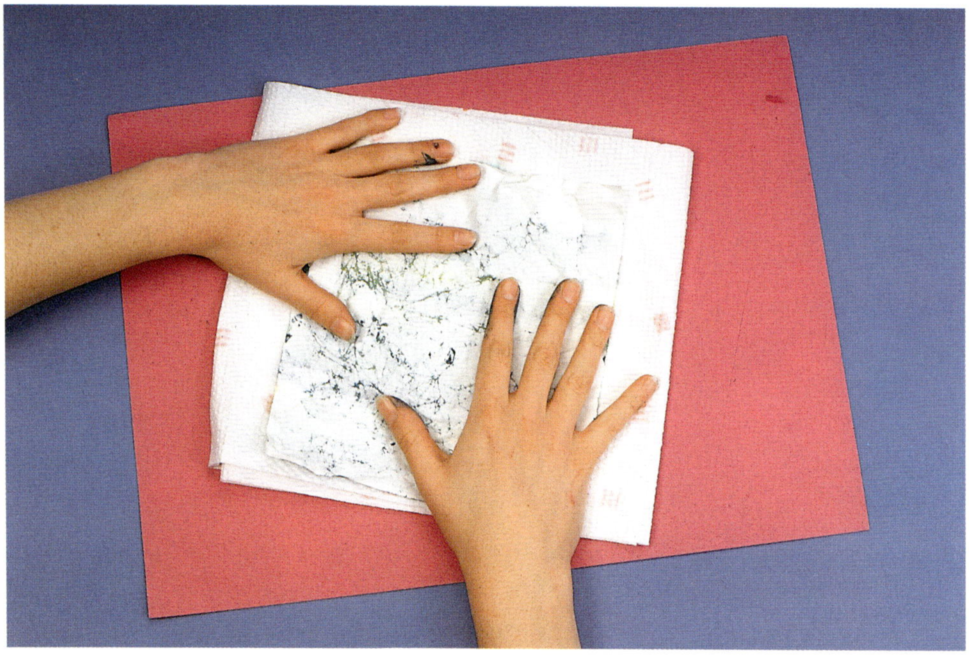

**9** Make a pad of two or three sheets of paper towel and place it on top of your bench or table. On a stronger sheet of paper, paint some colored dots, circles, lines or other shapes with wet paint. While the paint is still wet, lay the sheet face down on to the pad and press down firmly.

**10** When you lift it up, it will leave a soft, printed image on the top sheet of paper towel.

Experiment with this crumpled paper technique to see how many different kinds of prints you can make.

# A collage landscape picture

A "relief" design is one in which attached materials – in this case paper – project (stick out) from the background surface.

You will need a variety of types of paper, a piece of strong paper or carboard or tagboard about 7″ x 9″ (18cm x 23cm) on which to create your collage, a pencil or felt-tipped pen and glue.

**1** Draw a series of lines freely across the base paper or cardboard with the pencil or felt-tipped pen. Leave varying spaces between the lines, ranging, say, from about 2.5cm to 5cm (1″ to 2″).

**2** Select six or seven different types of paper (newspaper, wrapping paper, wallpaper, for example). Tear strips of these different papers to fit into the spaces between the lines. You do not need to be absolutely accurate, but your aim should be to fill the spaces completely when the torn pieces are stuck down.

**3** Some areas could be colored in with the felt-tipped pen, or you might even like to texture them with little dots or scribbled marks.

**4** Draw or paint some trees on your collage picture to complete it.

# Making your own paper

The processes involved in making decorative sheets of paper by hand from recycled papers and plant materials are quite simple. You will, however, require the help of an adult or an older brother, sister or friend with some of the things you need to do. Work carefully so that you don't make a mess. If the weather is fine, I suggest that you work outside.

You will need two plastic buckets, a wooden spoon or stick for stirring, a small wooden frame called a *mold* (photos 1-5 show you how to make this) a selection of used paper ("dull," not shiny paper, e.g., tissue paper, envelopes, computer printout paper, paper bags, brown wrapping paper, cardboard egg cartons) and water.

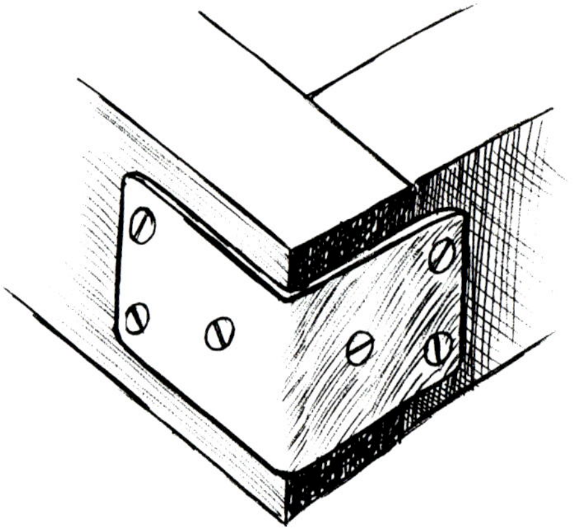

**1** Join the strips of wood together at the corners so that they form a *rectangular* frame (10" x 8", 25cm x 20cm). Use the L-shaped braces, as these will not rust and discolor your hand-made papers. Screw them into place.

**2** Now cover *one* side of the wooden frame with a piece of the net curtain. Its mesh may be fine or coarse and you can have fun experimenting with different types.

**3** Staple (or attach with thumbtacks) one edge of the net curtain to the underside of one edge of the frame. Now pull the net tightly across the frame and staple the opposite edge down firmly. Repeat this operation along the other two edges. The stretched net curtain should now be taut, like an artist's canvas.

## Making the "mold"

The mold, or wooden frame, needs to be strong and firm to give you the best possible results. You might find it useful to have some help in making this, to ensure that it is well constructed.

You will need a length (about 90cm, 3ft) of soft wood with a *square section* (for example, 1″ x 1″ (2.5cm x 2.5cm), or similar). This can be purchased from a lumberyard. This strip should be sawed into four lengths – two x 10″ (25cm) long and two x 8″ (20cm) long. (These lengths are only a guide and you may wish to change them.)

Soft wood is ideal for your first experiments in papermaking, though hard woods such as mahogany and teak are better for making molds which will get lots of use. Professional papermakers use hard woods for their molds.

You will also need small, L-shaped brass or aluminum braces, small brass screws, a screwdriver, some old net curtain material, and thumbtacks or a staple gun and staples.

You now need to make another, lighter wooden frame to fit on to your mold (see photos 4 and 5). For this you will need a length (about 3ft, 90cm) of soft wood with a square section (½″ x ½″, 1.2cm x 1.2cm). This length should be sawn into four sections, two x 10″ (25cm) and two x 8″ (20cm). Join the strips together as before, with braces and screws.

**4** Place this lighter frame on the net curtain side of your mold.

**5** Attach it with a few short strips of masking tape to hold it in place.

## Making a sheet of paper by hand

The method of papermaking described here is easy to follow.

**6** Tear up some of your pieces of used paper and place them in a plastic bucket.

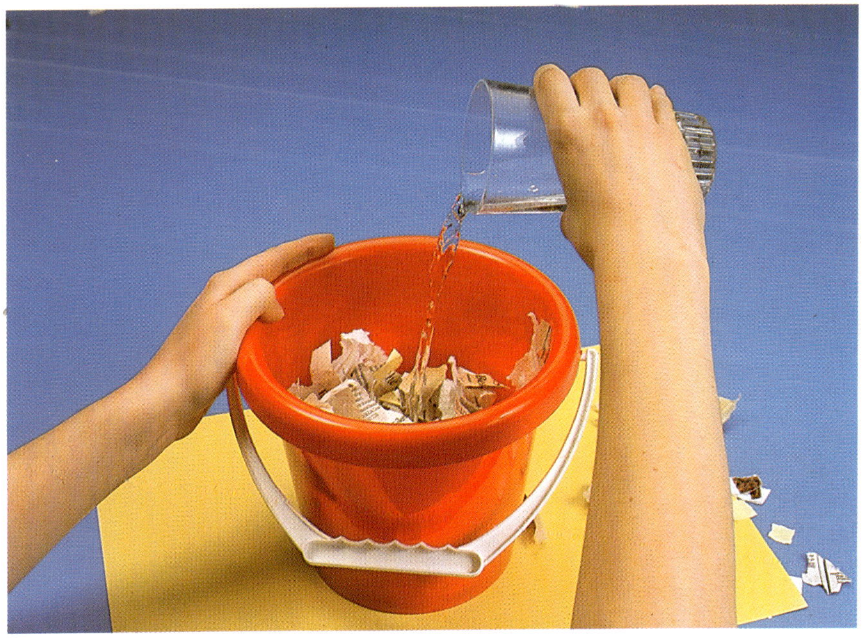

**7** Pour cold water over the torn-up paper and allow it to soak overnight. (If you are in a hurry, then you may, with care, use very hot water and leave the mixture for about two to three hours).

**8** Pound the soaked paper into a mushy, porridgelike pulp. You will need to stir it vigorously with the wooden spoon or stick.

**9** Rest your mold on top of the second bucket. Scoop up some of the pulp and place it into the mold.

**10** Use your hands to spread the pulp around carefully.

**11** Make sure that you cover the mesh right up to the edges. (You might be interested to know that in papermaking an edge is called a "deckel". Unlike a cut edge, it tends to be slightly ragged.)

**12** Leave the wet mush in the mold to dry before peeling it from the mold. (For further information on drying paper, see page 30.)

**An alternative method**
Pour the pulp into an old washing-up bowl.

Take your mold (mesh side down) and dip one of its shorter sides into the mushy pulp.

Slide the mold slowly underneath the surface of the pulp. (Note: If you follow this method, make sure the measurements of your mold allow it to fit into the washing-up bowl!)

Slowly scoop up some pulp in the mold.

Lift the mold out, allowing excess liquid to drain away.

In order to support the now heavy, wet mush of matted fibers, place the mold on a wire baking rack so that further drips of liquid fall away into a bucket or a sink. Leave to dry.

**13** This early print shows the papermaker scooping pulp from a huge, wooden vat with his mold.

**Useful hints**
**1** When making the pulp, you will get better results if your torn-up pieces of paper are small (say, ½″-1″, 1-2cm).
**2** Don't leave the pulp in a bucket for longer than two days, otherwise it will become smelly.
**3** Clean buckets and other equipment immediately after use.

**Experimental variations**

Paper is not only a material on which to draw, write, print or paint. It can be enjoyed simply as a decorative material which varies in color and texture. When producing your own sheets of handmade paper you can use a variety of raw materials to obtain effective variations in color, pattern and texture. Here are some ideas.

1 Add two or three leaves from plants to the pulp as you mix it.

2 Various flower-heads (daisies, dandelions, roses or daffodils, for example) can be squeezed in your fingers and then mixed into the pulp.

3 Try sprinkling a few seeds, small flower-heads or petals on to the damp layer of pulp in your mold so that when it dries they become part of the sheet of paper.

4 Add a little starch or gelatin to the pulp as you mix it, to give the paper more body. (This will also tend to give it a slightly smoother surface.)

5 Thin or sliced flower stalks will give an unusual effect.

6 Experiment with dried leaves, dried grasses and dried flowers.

7 Sprinkle some coffee or tea grains on to the damp layer of pulp in the mold.

8 Obtain color variations by adding to the pulp as you mix it some ink, paint, cold water dye, cold tea or cold coffee.

9 Drop a few spots of ink or paint on to the damp layer of pulp in the mold.

Try combining one or more of these ideas.

Keep a notebook in which you write about your experiments. Note down the various types of papers which you used to make your pulp; the different types of natural materials which you added; and how you obtained certain effects of color and texture. Glue small samples of the papers you have made beside your written notes.

As you become more skilled in making paper, you may wish to try a few clever variations. Here are some more ideas:

1 Make a quantity of very thick, dark-colored pulp. Keep it ready for use in a plastic bowl so that you can quickly add lumps of it to a thinner layer of lighter-colored pulp in the mold.

2 Drag your fingers through a layer of wet pulp in the mold to produce "ridges" and "furrows."

3 Place one or two delicate feathers into a layer of damp pulp in the mold.

14 Press and poke a layer of pulp which is almost dry so that areas of it are torn.

15 Sprinkle some delicate flower petals, leaves, seeds or grass stalks on to the pulp.

4 Place lengths of colored wool, string or cotton into a layer of damp pulp as it lies in the mold and then allow it to dry.

5 Do the same again but this time tear away some areas of the damp paper to produce interesting effects.

Photos 16-19 show the results of some of these ideas. Now try some ideas of your own.

16

17

18

### Drying a sheet of newly-made paper

A layer of wet pulp may be left in the mold to dry. This takes quite a long time, however, and you may wish your paper to dry quickly.

If so, place your mold, mesh side down, on a thick pad of newspaper or on an old blanket, if you have one. Such a pad will act like blotting paper and will soak up a lot of moisture from the layer of pulp.

After about an hour you should lift the mold off the pad and rest it on two strips of wood so that air is able to circulate beneath it. This will help the sheet of new paper to dry out more quickly.

The surface of your sheet of paper will be rough. You will be unable to write properly on it with pen and ink, but sometimes a felt-tipped pen may be used successfully.

Experiment by drawing and painting freely with different materials and tools.

19

# Making indented designs



Indented patterns are produced by impressing objects into the surface of a sheet of paper. The objects themselves must be hard and firm so that they will affect the paper by leaving "pressed" marks in it.

You will need a piece of strong cardboard or a cork tile, seeds or grains of sand, a sheet of paper, a sponge and a spoon.

**1** Sprinkle some seeds or grains of sand on to the cardboard or cork tile.

**2** Dampen the sheet of paper with the sponge and lay it down on the "seeded" surface. Rub the paper gently but firmly with the back of the spoon or with your hand. Lift up the paper and allow it to dry. Use your piece of indented paper in some exciting way by coloring it with crayon or dryish paint.

Here are some other ideas.
**1** Instead of rubbing the paper with a spoon, try putting a pad of newspaper over it, placing two or three heavy books on top and leaving it to dry.
**2** Take a sheet of paper, a spoon, a pad of newspaper and a ruler. Place the clean paper on the newspaper pad. Now draw a series of straight lines by using the blunt end of the spoon and the ruler. Press firmly into the paper.
**3** Instead of the spoon, use small twigs or cut-out cardboard shapes to impress patterns.
**4** Using seeds or grains of sand as shown in photo 1, make a pattern based upon circles.
**5** Try different methods, and use objects such as a wire baking rack, a plastic rack and string.

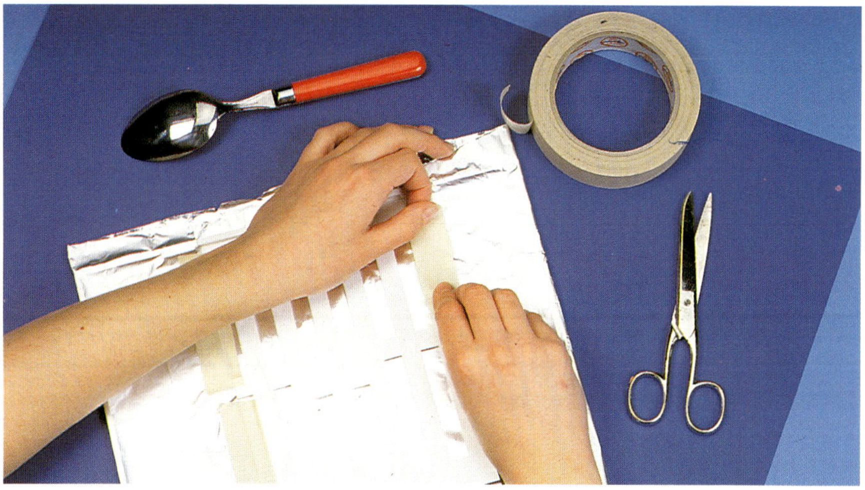

**3** Tape a design made from strips of cardboard on to a sheet of aluminum foil.

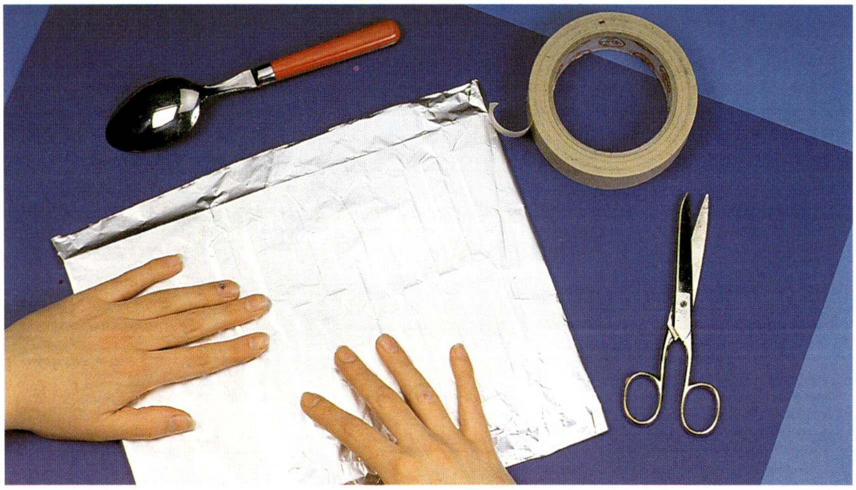

**4** Turn the sheet over and rub gently but firmly with the back of a spoon. The cardboard strips will form an indented pattern on the foil.

**5 and 6** What do you think was used to make these patterns?

5

6

# Papier – mâché dishes

Dish-like shapes made from paper are not difficult to make. You can start by using a rubber ball (a small soccer ball will do nicely), a plastic bucket (large enough for the ball to sit in the top), some paper (pieces of newspaper or wrapping paper), wallpaper paste, a paintbrush (1″, 2.5cm, household paintbrush), a plastic bowl or basin to hold the paste and some petroleum jelly.

**1** Place the rubber ball in the top of the bucket. Spread a thin coating of petroleum jelly over just less than half the ball's surface.

**2** Tear some pieces of paper into small strips. Place some wallpaper paste into a small dish. Dip the pieces of torn paper into the paste and put them on to the ball. Make sure you cover the area of the ball's surface which has been coated with petroleum jelly. Now brush paste over the paper-covered surface of the ball and add a second layer of torn paper pieces. Make these overlap. If time permits, allow these two layers to dry. Continue to add further layers (five or six layers will be sufficient). Allow the pasted paper to dry completely.

**3** When the adhesive has dried out and the papier-mâché bowl seems to be firm, gently remove it from the rubber ball. It will have an irregular rim. You may wish to leave this as a decorative feature, otherwise cut it with scissors to make it straighter. Decorate your bowl with painted patterns.

4 Make a papier-mâché dish using a lemon (or orange) instead of a rubber ball.

5 Make a small animal from your papier-mâché dish.

6 Paint in its eyes and use some string for its tail.

**7** Make a papier-mâché mask using a pottery bowl as your mold.

**8** Paint the inside of your bowl shape blue, and trim it with a pair of scissors.

**9** Paint on a face.

**10** Cut strips of orange paper.

**11** "Curl" the strips of paper. Hold a paper strip between your thumb and first finger and carefully pull the edge of a blunt knife or pen along the paper.

**12** Fasten the curled strips to your mask with sticky tape, to represent hair.

**13** The finished mask.

**14** This is another simple mask. It was large enough to wear, so small holes were made in the eyes and it was held in place by a rubber band.

**15** Decorate a papier-mâché pot with paint.

**16** After painting the inside white, add blue dribbles.

**17** Formal patterns may also be used, while aluminum foil will produce different effects.

**18** This delicate green and blue bowl was inspired by a bird's egg.

**19** Try combining two bowls to produce a different shape.

**1** Using a Stanley knife (or X-acto knife) and metal ruler, cut some patterns into fairly strong paper.

**2**

**2** and **3** These pictures will give you some pattern ideas.

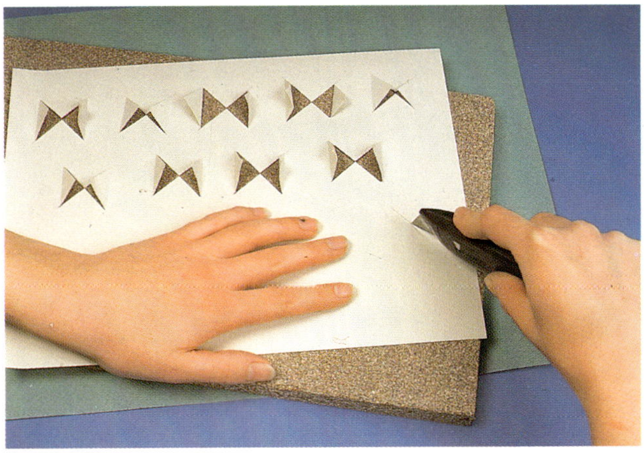

**3**

**4** Try raising up parts of the patterns for effect.

**5** and **6** Why not produce simple standing structures to look like buildings or sculptures?

**5**

**6**

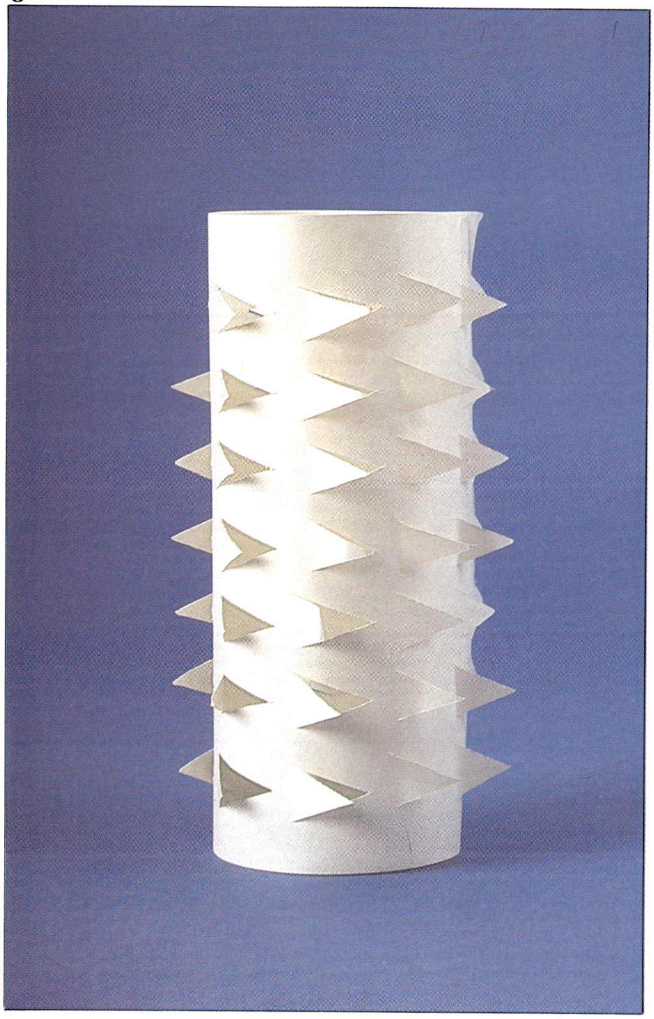

**7** Make more torn paper pattern reliefs with plain white and colored paper. Add some pieces torn from magazine photographs for effect.

**8** Twist some of the paper strips to make one of your patterns different.

**9** Design three cut paper patterns based upon squares.

Now go on to be much more inventive. Experiment freely. Develop some of the ideas you have already tried out. Mount your work neatly on stiff card or colored paper and display it.

# Further information



Most of the materials mentioned in this book are easy to obtain. Some are simply scrap materials and will cost you nothing. Others, like paints, magic markers and adhesives, can be purchased from stationers and/or artists' materials shops. A visit to an arts and crafts store will provide you with items like wood, paintbrushes and cheap plastic buckets. Materials in large quantities can be ordered through a schools' supplier.

**Some helpful books**

BOTTOMLEY, Jim, *Paper Projects for Creative Kids of All Ages,* Little Brown & Co., 1983.

FOWLER, Virginia, *Paperworks: Colorful Crafts from Picture Eggs to Fish Kites,* 1985.

CORWIN, Judith Hoffman, *Papercrafts,* Franklin Watts, 1988.

SMITH, Elizabeth Simpson, *Paper,* Walker & Company, 1984.

GUMMER, Arnold E., *Paper by Kids,* Dillon, 1980.

BODGER, Lorraine, *Paper Dreams,* Universe, 1977.

CAMPBELL, Margaret W., *Paper Toy Making,* Dover, 1975.

GRATER, Michael, *Complete Book of Paper Mask Making,* Dover, 1984.

GRATER, Michael, *Make It in Paper: Creative Three-Dimensional Paper Projects,* Dover, 1983.

# Index